KEONI'S BIG QUESTION

Patti B. Ogden
Illustrated by Mary Manning

KEONI'S BIG QUESTION

CAPSTONE PRODUCTIONS LLC
6103 S. Hickory Rd
Oregon, IL 61061

A member of the Christian Small Publishers Association

www.capstone-productions.com
info@messagekidsbooks.com

ISBN 13: 978-0-9816783-6-8
First Edition

Printed in the United States of America

Inspired from sermons of William Marrion Branham.

Keoni (Key-Oh-Knee) is the Hawaiian version of John.

Special thanks to Larry Harrah

Library of Congress Control Number: 2008906692

Ogden, Patti
Keoni's BIG Question / by Patti B. Ogden
Illustrated by Mary Manning
Summary: A young boy who seeks answers about
God's presence in every day life finds his friend held the key to
his revelation all along.

Children's Religious Fiction

Dedicated to the little ones that fill my life with joy;

Ezra, Levi, Micah and Isabelle Grace

The small green dinghy traveled silently around the first bend of the Ohio River and glided easily under a lush canopy of colorful hardwood trees. The maple, birch, aspen and oak trees seemed to be crying tears of joy that morning, as the last of the midnight rain dripped off the tips of the leaves and dropped into the river water below. Keoni watched as the drops made circles in the still waters near the bank. The sun had just popped its head up over the eastern horizon, and the birds were singing their sunrise praises among the dew soaked flowers.

It had been a long, dry summer, and the lack of rain had lowered the level of the Ohio River – but not enough to hinder the fishermen. It wasn't much farther until the boat would reach its destination, a perfect fishing spot called Six Mile Island. Keoni loved to go there with his friend Old Fisherman. Each summer, ever since he could remember, he was invited to go along with the white bearded, Christian gentleman who lived next door to Keoni's family. His wife had gone on to glory some time ago and Keoni's family looked after him, and loved him, as one of their own.

Old Fisherman had taught Keoni all about fishing. He shared his knowledge of rod and reel, how to bait, hook, tie on a weight and attach bobbers. But most importantly, the kind old man taught Keoni how to wait quietly and patiently for the fish to bite. Keoni knew how to be quiet. But today, he was exceptionally quiet.

Old Fisherman kept rowing the oars. "Clip, Clip, Clip," the oars hit the water in a rhythmic pattern. He studied Keoni's face carefully. He could tell something was bothering the little lad, but years of wisdom told him not to say anything just yet.

A sudden rustling noise startled them both. It was coming from under some old fallen limbs near the waters edge. A mother duck and her fuzzy yellow ducklings popped out from under the leaves and into plain view but quickly swam away from the approaching boat. Keoni smiled a bit. There was never a shortage of beautiful wildlife when he was on the river. Often they would see deer, beaver, squirrels and chipmunks on their journey. One time they spotted a majestic eagle soaring high in the sky.

Keoni loved being on the water. In fact, he loved nature. He never mentioned it to anyone really, but playing outside, especially fishing with his friend, made him very happy and content. Yet today was different. Keoni was troubled. He had a question – a really BIG question. A question so big that no one could answer it… at least to his satisfaction; and he wondered if he would ever find the answer!

Sure, most people tried to answer his question. Some people acted like they knew the answer. Some people admitted they just didn't know. Others just ignored him or shooed him away, and a few people just said "No." But no just didn't seem to be the right answer to Keoni.

Keoni had listened intently to the sermons each Sunday during church. The preaching had been so powerful lately and the anointing in the congregation had made him feel like Almighty God could be right there with them walking the aisles. He was so interested in learning about a God whose Word was as sharp and powerful as a two-edged sword!

Keoni had also felt the love that the brethren had shown to his family, even when they were new and didn't know much about the Bible.

One Sunday after service, Keoni asked the pastor "I have heard you talk about how great and wonderful God is and I was wondering…can anyone see God?"

"Why, certainly not, son." The pastor said. "No one can see God."

The next week, Keoni asked his Sunday school teacher. "Teacher, can anyone see God?"

"No," said the teacher, "God is so great but no one can see him."

Keoni was still very curious, so he asked his friends one day while they were running in the park. "Do you think anyone can see God?" "No way," said his friends who ran even faster. Keoni decided they must not want to talk about serious things during play time.

No just didn't seem to be the right answer to Keoni. He made up his mind that the answers he received were the kind people give when they really don't know how to approach a big question like that. Someone has to know, he thought. He just couldn't get it off his mind.

One night in bed Keoni lay gazing at the big full moon outside his window. He saw the stars twinkling so bright. "They are so great and wonderful," thought Keoni "and I can see them. Why can't I see God?"

Mother came in to tuck him in. "Mama, if God is as great as you said He is, why can't we see God?"

"Oh," sighed Mother, as she fluffed his pillow and smoothed the blankets up under his arms, "you'd best ask the pastor a question like that, he can explain it better. I am not able to tell you that, son." Mother kissed him tenderly. Keoni closed his eyes and never let his Mama know his disappointment. His had already asked the pastor. Now, what? How would he ever find out the real answer to his question?

Now here he was in the boat with Old Fisherman and his mind was still unsettled. They reached Six Mile Island and began to fish. The pair caught a nice mess of croppies and bluegill before Keoni noticed the sky becoming dark over to the west. Old Fisherman never said a word but began to put the tackle and bait away as he kept an eye on the sky.

"Lad, I think it best to find some cover. It is fixing to rain for a spell," he said. Rowing to shore hastily, they jumped onto the bank and Old Fisherman secured the fishing gear and anchored the boat just before a loud clap of thunder roared and rain let loose like buckets of water from heaven. "It's coming down hard!" shouted Keoni, "we are going to get soaking wet."

The two ran as fast as they could and found refuge under a thicket of pine trees. Old Fisherman had grabbed an old piece of canvas out of the boat and they formed it into a small shelter. He held tight to Keoni. "Hopefully, it will be over soon," comforted Old Fisherman. The wind shifted suddenly and began to blow even stronger. Big waves slammed the boat against the rocks on the bank. The sky turned pitch black and it rained harder. Keoni had always been afraid of storms, they sounded so scary and threatening. At home in his bed he would find peace by hiding under his blankets. Now, here he was in the midst of a raging storm and oh how he wished for the comfort of his own bed again!

"CRASH! CRACK!" another piercing clap of thunder, and then a blinding bolt of lightning came so close that Keoni let out a scream. "I am…scared!" cried Keoni. He felt his body begin to tremble, and the more he tried to stop it, the harder he shook. Oh, how he just wanted to go home! Keoni looked up at his friend and noticed his eyes were closed. He wondered if he might be saying a prayer. He remembered what his mother told him about prayer. "Keoni," she would say, "If you ever need God to help you, just pray from your heart and He will fill your need." Well, if there was ever a time of need, this was it, he decided. He said a silent prayer and asked God to calm the storm so they could get home safely.

"CRASH! BANG!" screamed the thunder. The lightning that quickly followed lit up the sky long enough for them to see the fishing boat beginning to sink under the weight of a fallen tree limb. "Oh, no, the boat!" shouted Old Fisherman as he ran toward the bank. He glanced back and with a firm voice said, "Son, you stay put." Keoni couldn't help feeling even more upset that now he wasn't only stuck in a storm, he had to stand all alone too! He watched nervously as Old Fisherman braved the pounding rain and pulled the tree limb off the boat. Keoni decided to pray even harder. "Please Lord, I need you," he sobbed.

With a quick yank on the side of the small boat, Old Fisherman had managed to get it afloat once more. By then, the rain had finally slowed down and he got enough of a foothold on the rocky bank to relieve its floor of river water. Old Fisherman sat down on a rock to catch his breath. The rain stopped. He looked back at Keoni, his face flushed with relief. "I think it's over now."

Keoni cautiously came out from under the canvas shelter. He looked warily at the sky. It did seem lighter. "No more thunder or lightning?" he asked. "No more," comforted Old Fisherman with his arms outstretched. Keoni made a mad dash towards his friend and hugged him tight. He made Keoni feel so safe. The pair quickly climbed into the boat. Keoni, taking his seat in the stern, was anxious to head home, while Old Fisherman lifted the anchor and pulled the oars into his lap and began rowing, once in a while looking over his shoulder.

The sun was going down in the west, and
the sky had cleared up for the most part.
The dark and gloomy clouds had disappeared,
and the ones that were left had turned into
fluffy puffs of purple and pink. Keoni felt
secure and happy enough by now to begin
daydreaming of how the fluffy clouds reminded
him of the cotton candy his mother allowed him
to buy once a year at the town fair. Gazing at the
clouds, he noticed a rainbow appearing in the
eastern sky. He began to alert Old Fisherman
of his discovery when he noticed his friend
had already been looking in that direction
and must have seen the rainbow long before
he ever spotted it. Old Fisherman was staring
at the rainbow and he was crying!

Keoni sat very still in the stern of the boat, looking at his friend. Tears were running down his cheeks and dripping onto his great white beard. At first Keoni was puzzled at why a grown up man would cry about a rainbow. Then, suddenly, he was intrigued by a thought that had never occurred to him before – after all these years of knowing Old Fisherman, a gentle, kind, Christian man, Keoni had never thought to ask him the big question!

It was so thrilling that he jumped up and ran to the center of the boat and knelt down at the old man's feet. "Sir, can I ask you a question that seemingly no one can answer?" Keoni never waited for a response, he just quickly continued, "can anyone see God?"

Old Fisherman was so overcome with the enthusiasm of the child, he pulled his oars into his lap and wept. He grabbed Keoni and put his arms around him. "God bless your little heart. All I've ever seen for the past forty years has been God. God is not very far away at all. He's right here. He's in his creation, He's in nature, He's in His Word and He's in His people. You see, the way you see God is to get God in the inside, then you can see right. When you know Him, you can understand and He will reveal Himself."

Keoni was stirred with all kinds of emotions. He really did understand! A new dawning took place inside of him, like the day when he finally understood the math problem on the school blackboard – when before it only looked like a jumble of numbers. He understood! Suddenly he realized he could see God. He had seen God! Keoni had so much joy he could hardly contain himself.

"You mean I have seen God in the stars?"

"Yes!" answered his friend.

"And I have seen God when the moon looks at me at night in bed?"

"Absolutely!" said Old Fisherman.

"And I see God in church?"

"Of course!"

"And I saw God calm the storm today and then give us this rainbow?" said Keoni, even more excited then before.

"Now you got it!" said Old Fisherman, "you see, if God is hid, He's hid to those whose eyes are blinded to Him."

"Praise God! I can see Him." shouted Keoni, smiling so hard at his friend he thought his face would crack. The two exchanged a look of complete understanding. No more words were necessary.

Keoni sat down and Old Fisherman rowed the oars hard the rest of the way.

When at last they walked up the sidewalk to Keoni's house, both felt delighted to be safe back home. How would they even begin to tell Keoni's mother of the events of the day? Old Fisherman held the door open for his little friend. Keoni paused and looked up. "Sir, may I tell you one more thing?"

"Sure, lad, what is it?"

"You told me that we can also see God in His people."

"Yes…"

"I just wanted you to know," said Keoni, "I have seen God in you."

In the words of
William Marrion Branham...

All of our books were inspired and written using stories, excerpts and actual sentences from the sermons of William Branham. It is our belief that Brother Branham received revelation and visions from the Lord Jesus Christ of what actually happened down throughout Bible history. Many of his personal stories are also told, we believe, to inspire spiritual growth so that we would personally know the character and loveliness of our savior. It is our mission and hope that you and your family will be blessed by these wonderfully unique books.

Coming soon from MessageKids™ Books
Shamgar and The Ox Goad
Momma, Am I Pretty?